SCHOLASTIC

Let's Find Out

My REBUS Reader

I0890029

Mailing a Holiday Card

by Kerilyn Acer

SCHOLASTIC INC.
New York Toronto London Auckland Sydney New Delhi Hong Kong

I put the card in my  .

mailbox

A  picks it up.

mail carrier

The mail gets sorted at the .

post office

My card goes on a  to Grandpa's town.

plane

A mail carrier puts it in Grandpa's  .

mailbox

Grandpa got my card! Happy holidays!

Let's Look at a Mailbox

When the mailbox arm is up, the mail carrier knows there is a letter inside that you want to send. Which mailbox has a letter for the mail carrier?

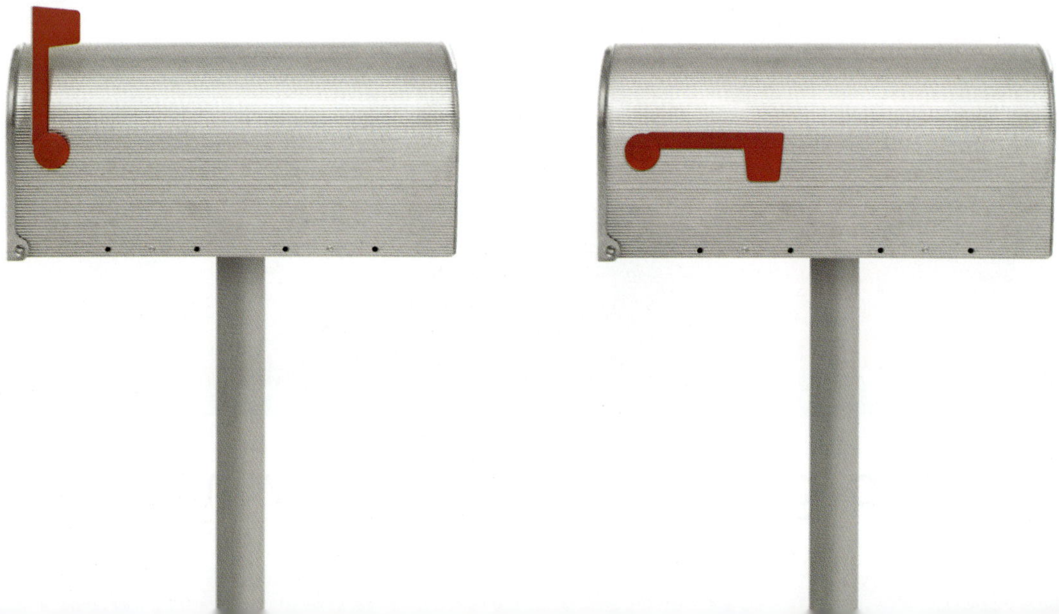